Industrial Railways
of the
British Isles

VOLUME 1 ~ STEAM

by Kevin Lane

Oxford Publishing Co. Oxford

Plate 1 On a fine June evening in 1967 a Vulcan Foundry 0-6-0ST (Builder's number 5299/date 1945) is seen at Houghton Colliery served by a branch of the Lambton Railway, Co. Durham. Rail traffic ended here in 1975, although No. 5299 was scrapped in 1972.

Rodney Wildsmith

© Oxford Publishing Co. 1979
SBN 86093 075 0

Typesetting by
Katerprint Co. Ltd., Oxford

Printed by
B.H. Blackwell in the City of Oxford

Published by
Oxford Publishing Co.
8 The Roundway
Headington
Oxford

Plate 2 One could not afford to wait for decent weather ▶ when photographing working steam in 1978! Two of Polkemmet Colliery's Barclay Six-Wheelers, an 0-6-0ST (1175/1909) leading an 0-6-0T (1296/1912), charge out of the yard ready to attack the 1 in 34 up to the exchange sidings on 23rd January, 1978.

Author

CONTENTS

INTRODUCTION

INTRODUCTION

The Ayr to Dalmellington bus obligingly deposited me outside Dunaskin Washery. The celebrated Waterside system at last, and not a minute too soon as it turned out. On the way to the office the sun finally broke through, lifting the spirits as it did so. As I did the necessary in the office, signing along the dotted line, a steam locomotive could be heard grappling with an obviously heavy train. A mental sigh of relief always follows the first sign of the locomotive, which you have come miles to photograph actually in steam and working. So often these days, one arrives at a steam location only to have one's hopes demolished by finding all motive power quite cold and confined to the murky depths of their shed. Even more galling is to be informed by some well-meaning soul that they had been in use the day before! Worse still happened to me last year when the Austerity at a certain northern location had failed with injector trouble and had limped back to the shed, literally minutes prior to my arrival.

Returning our attention to Waterside, emerging into the warm winter sunshine all was revealed as black-liveried Barclay 2244 arrived hotfoot with the lengthy rake of fulls from Pennyvenie Colliery. A brief period of to-ing and fro-ing ensued as the train was split up, the various wagons being weighed and despatched to the appropriate sidings prior to the washing of their contents. This completed, 2244 scuttled away light engine. I later found her stabled beside the locomen's rest-room together with the day's other working locomotive, Barclay 2335, the Giesl fitted 0-6-0T. Here I illicited the information that both would be working up the line shortly.

They caught me up near to the closed, and now derelict Minnivey Mine, 2244 propelling side-tippers of dirt, hotly pursued by 2335 pulling Pennyvenie-bound empties. The two trains were running so close together that at first I concluded that they were coupled together and running as one. Not so however. As if at some pre-arranged spot 2244 accelerated ahead and on reaching the mine branched off and took her train down behind the ruined buildings to where her load of dirt was to be tipped. Meanwhile, a gasping 2335 took on water before continuing on to Pennyvenie. This pause gave the fireman an opportunity to shovel coal forward in the 'tender', in practice an old wooden-bodied coal wagon with the end nearest the engine removed.

After 2244 had left, to return to Dunaskin, I walked the mile or so to Pennyvenie in the wake of 2335.

Voluminous emissions of smoke from the locomotive pinpointed her whereabouts quite early on and by the time I had reached it the train was just about ready to leave, with, as it subsequently turned out, the last load of the day. I was resigned to one or two shots of the departure followed by the trek back to Dunaskin. I hadn't reckoned with the driver however, who invited me up onto the footplate for the return journey. Standing in the stuffy and surprisingly commodious cab, ankle deep in coal, hammering along the beautiful sunlit Doon valley was indeed an experience to remember for a long, long time. This was *real* working steam, doing the job it was built to do, something even our best preserved lines cannot hope to recreate.

Six months later the line closed, the lifting of the 'main line' taking place during the Summer of 1978. All that remained of the railway, the Washery area at Dunaskin, came under the control of the Opencast Executive and was renamed Benbain Disposal Point. A Sentinel diesel was brought in to handle the remaining traffic.

Despite the closure, the above sketch does illustrate the point, that contrary to popular opinion, working steam *did not* come to an end in 1968. Compared with the present (1979) situation there was a superabundance of it around then. Choice examples included the Wemyss Private Railway, the National Coal Board systems at Lambton, Maesteg, Whitehaven, and Backworth, the celebrated Doxford crane tanks, and certain privileged parts of London who were to have their skys darkened by London Transport's dwindling fleet of ex-G.W.R. pannier tanks for nearly another three more years.

Ten years on however, the industrial steam locomotive is hanging on literally by its fingertips. Probably the best area to catch it in action would appear to be Scotland. Despite the recent losses of Kinniel Colliery and the Waterside railway, quite a variety can still be found, at Polkemmet, Frances and Bedlay collieries together with the Sentinels at Whifflet Foundry and the lone Barclay fireless at the Shell refinery at Ardrossan. Other locomotives exist of course, either in the capacity of spares to diesels or dumped out of use pending scrapping or, if lucky, preservation.

South Wales, another traditional steam stronghold, has been reduced to the Mountain Ash system and Brynlliw Colliery on a regular basis, together with a couple of fireless examples. (How many of the thousands of visitors who have flocked to Mr. Woodhams' establishment over the years know of the regularly used Barclay fireless next door at Sully?) Again, a few other locomotives can, from time to time, be found in steam but none can be relied upon to put up a regular showing.

Pockets of resistance elsewhere in Britain include Bersham Colliery in North Wales, Bold Colliery, plus one or two power stations. Astonishingly, at the time of writing, only one non-N.C.B. location, Castle Donington Power Station, can regularly be expected to steam a conventional (i.e. not Sentinel or fireless) locomotive.

The photographs in this album have been carefully selected to illustrate the industrial steam locomotive at work over the past five years, and above all to bring across the unique atmosphere of the industrial steam worked railway. Locomotive close-ups have largely been omitted as the various types have been adequately covered elsewhere. Hopefully, I have whetted a few appetites with the photographs within. If so, the best advice I can give is hurry up!

In conclusion, I would like to offer my sincerest thanks to the following people who have made this album possible:— The various photographers who have answered my call for material, namely Victor C.K. Allen, A.J. Booth, T.G. Flinders, P.J. Fowler, J.G. Glover, Joe Rajczonek, E.C. Salthouse, Graham F. Scott-Lowe, R.E.B. Siviter and Rodney Wildsmith. Further thanks are due to Adrian Booth who also checked my captions and gave general helpful criticism, and the various locomotive owners who have allowed us onto their premises and to their staff (particularly the long suffering N.C.B.). Also to the Industrial Railway Society who have done so much with their indispensable publications to further the interest in industrial railways.

Kevin Lane
Dunstable
June 1979.

SCOTLAND

Plate 3 With snow on her boots, No. 9 a Hudswell, Clarke 0-6-0T (895/1909) shuffles through the yard at Bedlay Colliery, just outside Glasgow on 19th January, 1978.

Author

Plate 4 In 1978 a rare sight indeed, in this country at least, two working Sentinel steam locomotives. On 19th January, 1978 *Denis* (9631/1958) and *Ranald* (9627/1957) pose in the snow between duties at R.B. Tennent Ltd's., Whifflet Foundry, Coatbridge, near Glasgow.

Author

SCOTTISH SENTINELS

Plate 5 *Ranald* seen running through the snow later the same afternoon. Two other similar Sentinel locomotives are owned by the company, *John* (9561/1953) and *Robin* (9628/1957).

Author

Plate 6 Early morning at Kinneil Colliery, overlooking the Firth of Forth at Bo'ness. No. 6 Barclay 0-4-0ST (2043/1937) ambles around the yard at half light on 24th January, 1978.

Author

Plate 7 Later the same morning, No. 6 looking very purposeful, propels wagons towards the stockpiles at Kinneil Colliery.

Author

POLKEMMET

Plate 8 Blast off! Barclays 0-6-0ST (1175/1909) and 0-6-0T (1296/1912) struggle up to the exchange sidings at Polkemmet Colliery, Lothian, on 23rd January, 1978. No need to tip the drivers if you want smoke effects here!

Author

Plates 9 and 10 Above. Polkemmet Colliery, where double heading is the norm, has become almost a legend amongst railway enthusiasts in recent years. On this occasion a Barclay 0-6-0ST (1175/1909) and a Giesl fitted 0-6-0T (1296/1912), near the BR exchange sidings and (Left) pass the engine shed with a Barclay 0-6-0ST (2358/1954) residing outside. 23rd January, 1978.

Author

Plate 11 On 20th January, 1978 a Barclay 0-4-0ST (2259/1949) shunts at Frances Colliery, Dysart, near Kirkaldy, Fife.

Author

Plate 12 A loaded train of coal hauled by a BR class 20 diesel receives a welcome push out of Frances Colliery by a Barclay 0-4-0ST (2259/1949) on 20th January, 1978.

Author

Plate 13 The largest concentration of industrial steam locos in Scotland in recent years lay dumped in a scrapyard near Thornton in Fife. The more presentable members, seen here on 20th January, 1978, are gathered in a line near the entrance. Former Wemyss Private Railway Barclay 0-6-0ST No. 15 (2183/1945) is at the far end followed by three 0-4-0ST's also from Barclays, and, nearest the camera, a Grant, Ritchie 0-4-0ST (272/1894) withdrawn from the nearby Rothes Colliery in 1969.

Author

STEAM FOR SCRAP

Plate 14 A memory of the Wemyss Private Railway adorning the tanks of this Barclay 0-6-0ST.

Author

WATERSIDE

Plate 16 As Barclay 0-4-0ST No. 10 approaches the photographer on 25th January, 1978, the shunter climbs down prior to stabling No. 10's train at Dunaskin Washery on the NCB Waterside system.

Author

Plate 17 While Giesl fitted Barclay 0-6-0T. No. 24 (2335/1953) shunts at Dunaskin Washery on 25th January, 1978, Barclay 0-4-0ST No. 10 prepares to go 'on shed'.

Author

Plate 18 No. 10 rests inside the shed at Dunaskin.

Author

Plate 19 Situated between Dunaskin Washery and Pennyvenie Colliery is Minnivey mine, closed in 1975. The site was latterly used as somewhere to tip dirt. Barclay 0-4-0ST No. 10 (2244/1947) performs this duty on 25th January, 1978.

Author

Plate 20 Out on the 'main line' at Minnivey en-route to Pennyvenie with empties from Dunaskin, No. 24 pauses for water, giving the fireman a chance to shovel coal forward into the loco tender from the back truck, a characteristic feature of this railway.

Author

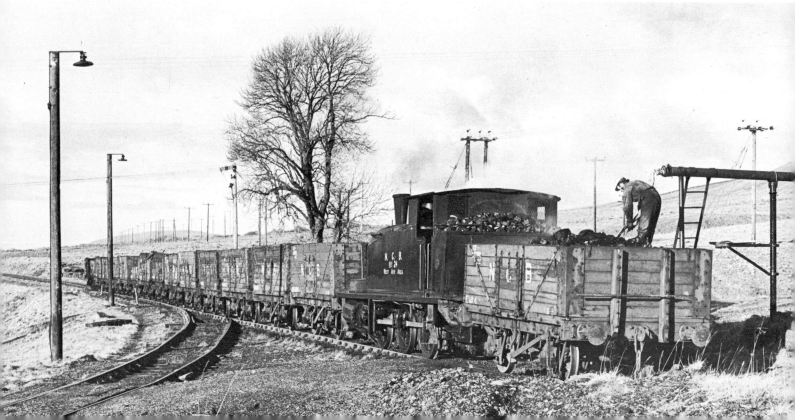

Plate 21 No. 10 propels side-tippers full of dirt for emptying at Minnivey.

Author

Plate 22 After a water stop, No. 24 draws her train of empties forward to Pennyvenie Colliery on 25th January, 1978, a little over six months before closure of the line.

Author

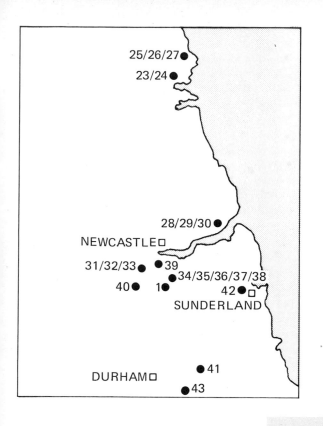

THE NORTH EAST

◄ *Plate 23* Vulcan Foundry 0-6-0ST No. 33 (5306/1945) picks her way through the trees along the line near Whittle Colliery, Northumberland.

E. C. Salthouse

Plate 24 Snow, steam . . . and sheep! A brief ovine invasion halts traffic on the Whittle Colliery branch.

E. C. Salthouse

Plate 25 Shilbottle Colliery was another steam outpost in Northumberland, not far in fact from Whittle illustrated on the previous page. In 1972 No. 45, an 0-6-0ST built by Robert Stephenson and Hawthorns (7113/43) is silhouetted as she works between the mine and the exchange sidings.

Joe Rajczonek

Plate 26 No. 45 again, leaving the colliery yard in January 1972.
E. C. Salthouse

Plate 27 On a beautiful summer's evening, Hunslet 0-6-0ST No. 48 (3172/1944) drifts towards Shilbottle Colliery with a train of empties.

E. C. Salthouse

Plate 28 No. 47, a Robert Stephenson and Hawthorns 0-6-0ST (7849/55) shunts at Backworth Colliery situated on the northern outskirts of Newcastle.

Victor C. K. Allen

Plate 29 In 1974 Robert Stephenson and Hawthorns 0-6-0ST No. 16 (7944/1957) brings a rake of empties up from the exchange sidings bound for Fenwick Colliery on the Backworth system.

Joe Rajczonek

BACKWORTH

Plate 30 No. 44, a Robert Stephenson and Hawthorns 0-6-0ST (7760/1953) returns to the shed at Backworth in May 1967. The line under the bridge is BR owned. Backworth was the last steam-worked shed in Northumberland, dieselization not completed until 1976.

Rodney Wildsmith

Plate 31 Derwenthaugh loco shed on the Tyne's south bank serves Derwenthaugh coking plant and Clockburn Drift. Now totally dieselized, steamier days are recalled by a decidedly grubby Austerity 0-6-0ST entertaining a group of 'Gricers' near the coking plant.

E. C. Salthouse

DERWENTHAUGH

Plate 32 Silhouetted by her own smoke, No. 24, Vulcan Foundry 0-6-0ST (5291/1945)* advances through the yard at Clockburn Drift in July 1967.

Rodney Wildsmith

Plate 33 After leaving the industrial sprawl of Derwenthaugh, the line to Clockburn Drift is surprisingly rural. In July, 1967 No. 24 is again pictured, here running alongside the river Derwent taking empties to Clockburn Drift.

Rodney Wildsmith

*An unidentified 0-6-0ST.

Plate 34 Vulcan Foundry 0-6-0ST No. 59 (5300/1945) and Robert Stephenson 0-6-2T No. 42 (3801/1920) catch the evening sun at the former Lambton Railway loco sheds at Philadelphia, Co. Durham in June 1967.

Rodney Wildsmith

Plate 35 No. 42 stretches her legs out on the old Lambton Railway near Philadelphia with coal empties for New Herrington Colliery in June 1967.

Rodney Wildsmith

Plate 36 Fully equipped signal boxes were indeed a luxury on industrial lines in this country. The one illustrated was to be seen at the Houghton Junction triangle where lines from New Herrington Colliery, Houghton Colliery and Lambton Coking Plant met. June 1967.
Rodney Wildsmith

PHILADELPHIA

Plate 37 In May 1967 Vulcan Foundry No. 59 approaches the box from New Herrington, with coal for Lambton Coking Plant.
Rodney Wildsmith

Plate 38 The inevitable end. Kitson 0-6-2T No. 31 (4533/1907) being cut up at Philadelphia. Awaiting its turn is No. 27, an 0-6-0T built originally by Robert Stephenson & Co. in 1846 as number 491 but rebuilt twice by the NER (in 1864 and 1873) and again at Lambton engine works in 1904.

Rodney Wildsmith

Plate 39 In 1968, Robert Stephenson and Hawthorns 0-4-0ST No. 81 (7604/1949) crosses the Team Valley with coal from Ravensworth Ann Colliery.

Rodney Wildsmith

Plate 40 Hunslet 0-6-0ST No. 83 (3688/1949) brings a full train out of Morrison Busty Colliery, Annfield Plain, in 1973 shortly before closure.

Joe Rajczonek

Plate 41 Hawthorn Leslie 0-6-0ST *Stagshaw* (3513/1927) makes an impressive job of propelling empties into Shotton Colliery yard in April 1967.

Rodney Wildsmith

Plate 42 One of the celebrated 0-4-0 crane tanks, *Hendon*, (Robert Stephenson and Hawthorns 7007/1940) at Doxford and Sunderland Ltd's Pallion shipyard.

Rodney Wildsmith

Plate 43 'Gone to Lunch' at Thornley Colliery; Barclay 0-4-0ST No. 52 (2275/1949).
Rodney Wildsmith

YORKSHIRE

◀ *Plate 44* On Christmas Eve 1977 a Hunslet 0-6-0ST *Monckton No. 1* (3788/1953) stands outside the roofless shed at North Gawber Colliery, Mapplewell.

A. J. Booth

Plate 45 Hudswell, Clarke 0-6-0T No. S100 (1822/1949) at Peckfield Colliery, Micklefield in October 1968.

Rodney Wildsmith

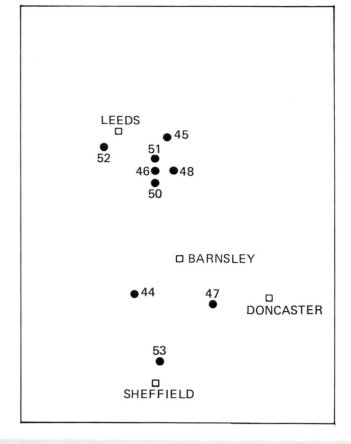

Plate 46 On 27th October, 1971 the scene at Wheldale Colliery, Castleford, with a Hunslet 0-6-0ST *Antwerp* (3180/1944) shunting empty wagons.

R. E. B. Siviter

Plate 47 Wilf Peckett 0-6-0ST No. 44 (1891/1940) is reflected in a large puddle at Manvers Main loco shed, which serves the coal preparation plant at Wath-upon-Dearne. An Austerity 0-6-0ST is stabled further on.

Rodney Wildsmith

Plate 48 Fryston No. 2 a Hudswell, Clarke 0-6-0T (1883/1955) makes a smoky appearance at Fryston Colliery on 17th September, 1971.

T. G. Flinders

Plate 49 In December 1968 a Hudswell, Clarke 0-6-0T *Elizabeth* (1600/1927) snorts up to the tip at Water Haigh Colliery.

Rodney Wildsmith

Plate. 50 Glasshoughton Colliery's 'Phantom Scribbler' has his opinions firmly disproved as this Hudswell, Clarke 0-6-0T No. S118 (1870/1953) moves out from under the shadow of the headgear in October 1968.

Rodney Wildsmith

Plate 51 "You should have seen it *before* we straightened it!" Hunslet 0-6-0ST *Astley* (3509/1947) makes inebriated progress along irregular looking track at Primrose Hill Colliery, Woodlesford, in December 1968.

Rodney Wildsmith

39

Plate 52 Keeping company with a pair of Class 88DS Rustons, a Barclay 0-4-0ST *Chemicals* (1823/1924) watches the world and a DMU go by at a scrapyard in Shipley, near Bradford in June 1978.

Author

Plate 53 On 27th June, 1976 Hunslet 0-6-0ST No. 2 (3888/1964) is seen shunting at Smithywood Coking Plant, Chapeltown, north of Sheffield.

A. J. Booth

THE NORTH WEST

WORKINGTON
61/62

●63

WHITEHAVEN
56/57/58/59/60

●64
66/67/68
MANCHESTER

●65

69
LIVERPOOL

CHESTER
●55
●54

Plate 54 With the preservation activities taking place further west, one is apt to forget that industrial steam still exists in North Wales. Bersham Colliery near Wrexham still plays host to two examples including *Hornet*, a Peckett 0-4-0ST (1935/1937) fitted with what appears to be a spark arrester. Photograph taken on 22nd March, 1977.

Author

Plate 55 Slightly north of Bersham was Gresford Colliery, closed in 1973. *Gwyneth*, a Robert Stephenson and Hawthorns 0-6-0ST (7135/1944) shunts wagons of dirt.

Joe Rajczonek

Plate 56 Solway No. 2 a Hudswell, Clarke 0-4-0ST (1814/1948) takes in the sea air at Whitehaven harbour in 1975 while shunting coal from Haig Colliery, having arrived via the Howgill incline.

Joe Rajczonek

Plate 57 The two ladies on Whitehaven station are doubtless immune to dirty tank engines, and chat away while *Solway No. 2* bustles past.

Joe Rajczonek

Plate 58 Before descending to Whitehaven harbour, coal from Haig Colliery is washed at Ladysmith Coal Preparation Plant. Hunslet 0-6-0ST *Stanley* (3302/1945) shunts coal from Haig whilst *King*, a giesl fitted Barclay 0-4-0ST (1448/19) attends to a line of stone wagons. This system, spectacular by any standards, closed in 1975.

Joe Rajczonek

Plate 59 Coal from Haig Colliery en-route to Ladysmith in 1974, with *Respite*, a Hunslet 0-6-0ST (3696/1950) in charge.

Joe Rajczonek

Plate 60 Hunslet 0-6-0ST *Repulse* (3698/1950) storms up the gradient towards Ladysmith Coal Preparation Plant with coal from Haig Colliery.

Joe Rajczonek

Plate 61 A rest for both crew and loco at Harrington Coal Preparation Plant, Lowca. The engine is *Amazon*, a Vulcan Foundry 0-6-0ST (5297/1945).

Joe Rajczonek

Plate 62 Hunslet 0-6-0ST *Warspite* (3778/1952) struggles to gain her feet with a load of coal for Harrington Coal Preparation Plant. *Amazon* waits for her turn.

Joe Rajczonek

Plate 63 British Gypsum Ltd's Barclay ▶ 0-4-0ST (2134/1942) slogs out of their Kirkby Thore works, Westmorland, in July 1968.

Rodney Wildsmith

Plate 65 A 'No Nonsense' exit from Bickershaw Colliery, near Leigh, as Hunslet 0-6-0ST No. 8 (3776/1952) and Robert Stephenson and Hawthorns 0-6-0ST *Gwyneth*, (7135/1944) late of Gresford Colliery, double head a heavy train of air-braked hoppers up to the BR exchange sidings in 1977.

Joe Rajczonek

Plate 64 The graceful lines of Peckett 0-4-0ST *May* (1370/1915) catch the early morning sun as she pauses in her duties at Yates, Duxbury's Paper Mills, Heap Bridge, Lancashire, on 5th March, 1969.

J. G. Glover

Plate 66 One of a trio of similar locomotives at Agecroft Power Station, Manchester, *Agecroft No. 1* an 0-4-0ST built by Robert Stephenson and Hawthorns (7416/1948) shuffles off shed to commence shunting duties on 18th March, 1977.

Author

Plate 67 The locos at Agecroft are a familiar feature to ▶ passengers on the former L & Y line between Manchester and Bolton. Its close proximity is shown here with No. 25 140 heading north, passing *Agecroft No. 1* on 18th March, 1977.

Author

Plate 68 Agecroft No. 1 again on 18th March, 1977 outside its shed at Agecroft Power Station. Its two partners, both 0-4-0STs built by Robert Stephenson and Hawthorns—7681/1951 and 7485/1948 are undergoing repairs.

Author

Plate 69 Immaculate after overhaul in March 1977, the spare engine at Bold Colliery, St. Helens, Hunslet 0-6-0ST *Whiston* (3694/1950), is pictured inside her shed, shared with the regular diesel.

Author

SOUTH WALES

Plate 70 A somewhat squat looking Peckett 0-6-0ST No. 1426 (1426/1916) backs down onto wagons at Brynlliw Colliery, Grovesend, on 6th April, 1978.
Author

72/73/74/75 ●
70/71 ● 76
NEATH □
SWANSEA □
PONTYPRIDD □
CARDIFF □

85 ●
87 ●
80 ● 81/82/83/84 ●
86 ●
79 ●
88 ●
NEWPORT □
89/90 ●

BRISTOL □

Plate 71 Peckett 0-6-0ST No. 1426 bustles through the yard at Brynlliw Colliery on 6th April, 1978.

Author

Plate 72 The loco shed at Pontardulais, serving Graig Merthyr Colliery, has for some time been a popular 'Watering Hole' for enthusiasts visiting South Wales. On 23rd May, 1977 *Norma*, a Hunslet 0-6-0ST (3770/1952) and a Bagnall 0-6-0ST (2758/1944) prepare for a day's work.

Graham F. Scott-Lowe

Plate 73 By April 1978 Graig Merthyr Colliery was on the ▶ verge of closure and only one loco was required in the mornings alone. Bagnall 2758 waits to go off shed.

Author

Plate 74 On 6th April, 1978 Bagnall 2758 proceeds light engine down to the exchange sidings to pick up empties for the colliery at Graig Merthyr.

Author

Plate 75 A sight no longer to be seen: Bagnall 2758 slogs up the valley towards Graig Merthyr Colliery. *Author*

Plate 76 On 21st July, 1977 a Peckett 0-4-0ST (1345/1914) poses to an appreciative audience on the occasion of a visit by the Industrial Railway Society to the Clydach works of Inco-Europe Ltd. Although usually spare to a diesel she is occasionally steamed for visits such as these.

Author

MAESTEG

Plate 77 Banked at the rear by Hunslet 0-6-0ST *Maureen* (2890/1943—rebuilt as 3882/1962), Hunslet 0-6-0ST *Linda* (3871/1952) heads a train of coal from St Johns Colliery to the washery at Maesteg in 1972.

Joe Rajczonek

Plate 78 Hunslet 0-6-0ST *Pamela* (3840/1956) and *Linda*, also from Hunslet, work together at Maesteg in 1973.

Graham F. Scott-Lowe

Plate 79 Two Hunslet 'Austerities' work together in the rain at Nantgarw Coking Plant, Treforest, on 1st December, 1972.
Graham F. Scott-Lowe

Plate 80 The massive OQ class Peckett 0-6-0ST (2150/1954) shunting at Maerdy Colliery on 30th May, 1973.
Graham F. Scott-Lowe

Plate 81 Trio at Mountain Ash loco shed on 25th October, 1972. Left to right:— *The Earl* Peckett 0-6-0ST (1203/1910), No. 8 Hunslet 0-6-0ST (3880/1961—rebuilt from Robert Stephenson and Hawthorns 7139/1944), and *Sir John* Avonside 0-6-0ST (1680/1914).

R. E. B. Siviter

MOUNTAIN ASH

Plate 82 On 23rd May, 1977 a Hudswell, Clarke 0-6-0ST (1885/1955) shunts at Mountain Ash.

Graham F. Scott-Lowe

Plate 83 Hudswell, Clarke No. 1885 pictured near Aberaman Phurnacite Plant on a damp and misty day in January 1973.

R. E. B. Siviter

Plate 84 At Mountain Ash shed on 8th October, 1974, *Sir John* in his sixtieth year looks healthier than the Avonside 0-6-0ST *Lord Camrose* (2008/1930) behind him, some sixteen years his junior.

Graham F. Scott-Lowe

Plate 87 On 11th December, 1973, *Islwyn*, a Barclay 0-6-0ST (2332/1952) is seen pounding around Talywain Landsale yard, Abersychan near Pontypool.

65

Graham F. Scott-Lowe

Plate 88 Monsanto Chemicals, Newport, is the home of this
0-4-0 fireless, built by Barclay (1966/1929) seen on 15th
February, 1978.

Graham F. Scott-Lowe

Plate 89 This Kerr, Stuart 0-4-0WT (3063/1918) is dumped out of use at Fairfield-Mabey
Ltd, Engineers, Chepstow, on 4th March, 1975.

Graham F. Scott-Lowe

Plate 90 Apparently taking root, this
Neilson 0-4-0ST (2119/1876) is in a sorry
state at Fairfield-Mabey Ltd Engineers,
Chepstow on 4th March, 1975.
Graham F. Scott-Lowe

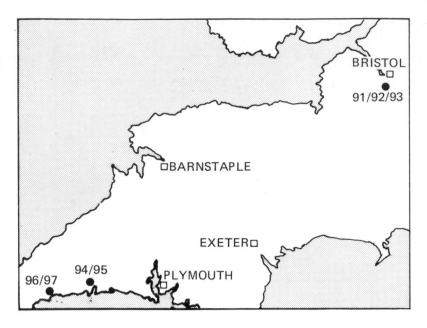

THE SOUTH WEST OF ENGLAND

Plate 91 On a cold winter's day a Peckett 0-4-0ST (1788/1929) is shunting at Kilmersdon Colliery, Radstock.

Graham F. Scott-Lowe

Plate 92 A loaded wagon from Kilmersdon Colliery starts the descent towards the BR North Somerset line.
P. J. Fowler

Plate 93 A general view of the Kilmersdon Colliery incline; the left hand (loaded) wagon is descending allowing an empty one to ascend by means of a rope attached to both wagons.

P. J. Fowler

Plates 94 and 95 Two views of *Judy* a Bagnall 0-4-0ST (2572/1937) photographed working at English China Clay's establishment at Par Harbour on 8th August, 1968. Her characteristic stunted appearance was enforced by the 7' 6" loading gauge clearance of some bridges under which she worked. This system has unfortunately recently closed although both *Judy* and sister (or should it be brother?) loco, *Alfred*, Bagnall 0-4-0ST (3058/1953) are destined for preservation.

R. E. B. Siviter

Plate 96 Hudswell, Clarke 0-4-0ST No. 5 (1632/1929) goes about her business at Falmouth Docks in March 1975.
Joe Rajczonek

Plate 97 Positively dwarfed by her surroundings, No. 5 trundles along the jetty at Falmouth Docks in March 1975.
Joe Rajczonek

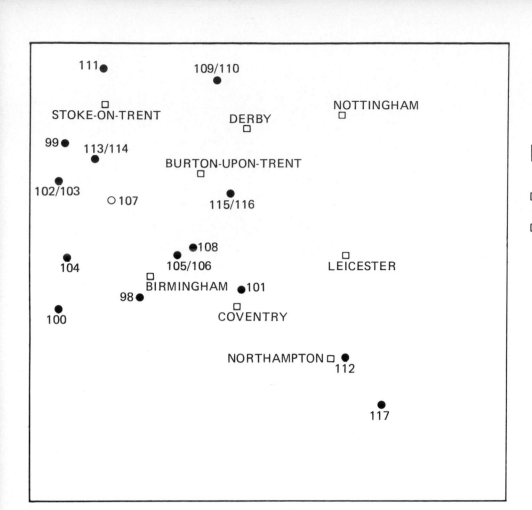

111 • 109/110 •

□ NOTTINGHAM □
STOKE-ON-TRENT DERBY
□

99 • 113/114 •
102/103 • BURTON-UPON-TRENT □

○ 107 115/116 •

•108
104 • 105/106
□ LEICESTER □
BIRMINGHAM •101
98 •

100 • COVENTRY □

NORTHAMPTON □ • 112

• 117

THE MIDLANDS

Plate 98 On 12th November, 1962 No. 1, an Avonside 0-4-0T (1977/ 1925) plays around with a single van at Cadbury's Bournville works, near Birmingham.

P. J. Shoesmith

Plate 99 Another line that recently finished with steam is that running from Littleton Colliery, Huntington, to BR exchange sidings at Penkridge. This 1976 view shows a Hudswell, Clarke 0-6-0ST (1752/44) getting to grips with a train of empties.

Joe Rajczonek

Plate 100 Barclay 0-4-0ST *Sir Thomas Royden* (2088/40) peeps over at the traffic below whilst propelling a train of coal empties out of Stourport Power Station on 20th March, 1972.

R. E. B. Siviter

Plate 101 In August 1969 former Western Region 0-6-0PT No. 1502 is in reflective mood at Coventry Colliery. ▶
Victor C. K. Allen

Plate 102 This Barclay 0-4-0 fireless (1944/1927) is busy beside the Stafford–Wolverhampton main line at Croda Synthetic Chemicals Ltd, Four Ashes, on 22nd April, 1978.
Author

Plate 104 Steamier days at Round Oak Steelworks, Brierley Hill. A begrimed Barclay 0-4-0ST *Billy* (1881/1925) shunts across Level Street in 1959, four years before being fed to the furnaces he served for 38 years.
P. J. Shoesmith

Plate 103 Barclay 1944 is seen again, under charge on 23rd April, 1978.

Author

Plates 105 and 106 Two views taken on 22nd April, 1978 of No. 9, a Robert Stephenson and Hawthorns 0-6-0T (7151/1944), working during an Industrial Railway Society visit to Hams Hall Power Station, Coleshill near Birmingham.

Author

Plate 107 Former Cannock and Rugeley collieries Lilleshall-built 0-6-0ST taking a loaded train down to the canal basin on the Cannock Wood system.

P. J. Shoesmith

Plate 108 One of Britain's more famous industrial locos, *William Francis*, a BP 0-4-4-0 Garrett, (6841/1937), steams up to Baddesley Colliery on a misty autumn morning in October 1965.

P.J. Shoesmith

Plate 109 Another well known loco, though rather due to age than appearance, *Holwell No. 3*, a Black Hawthorn 0-4-0ST (266/1873) shunts hoppers out of the BR sidings at Tarmas Roadstone Holdings Ltd's Wirksworth Limestone Quarry on 23rd July, 1971, in her 98th year.

R. E. B. Siviter

WIRKSWORTH

Plate 110 Peckett 0-4-0ST *Uppingham* (1257/1912) idly pushes a few wagons around at Wirksworth Limestone Quarry on 14th April, 1972.

R. E. B. Siviter

Plate 111 "Anyone for cricket?" Birchenwood Gas & Coke Co. Ltd, Bagnall 0-6-0ST No. 4 seen shunting on 26th July, 1972.

R. E. B. Siviter

Plate 112 In February 1970 this Hawthorn Leslie 0-4-0 fireless (3829/1932) is shunting full wagons at Northampton Power Station.

Joe Rajczonek

Plate 113 Topham, a Bagnall 0-6-0ST (2193/1922) shunts in a blizzard at West Cannock Colliery, Staffs, on 19th December 1969.

R. E. B. Siviter

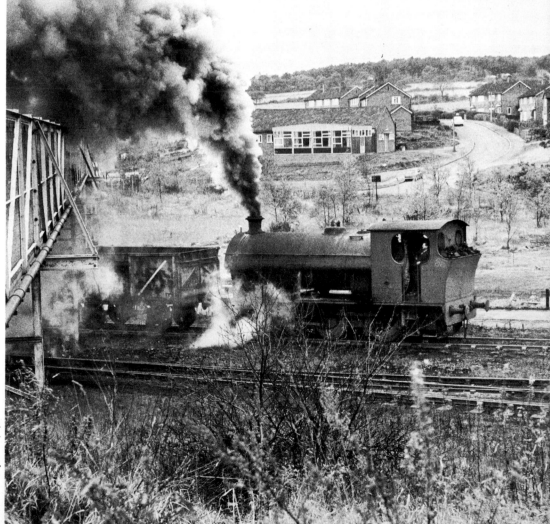

Plate 114 Topham at work on a somewhat better day in October 1969.

R. E. B. Siviter

Plate 115 A green liveried 'Austerity,' Cadley Hill No. 1, built by Hunslet (3851/1962) storms towards Cadley Hill Colliery, near Burton-on-Trent on 22nd September, 1977.

Author

Plate 116 Earlier the same day *Cadley Hill No. 1* was seen reversing into the landsale yard.

Author

Plate 117 Just another piece of scrap—a Hawthorn Leslie 0-6-0ST (3138/1915) and *left*, a partially hidden Barclay 0-6-0ST, (2138/1941) slumber in a scrap merchants yard near Wolverton, Buckinghamshire, in March 1974.

Author

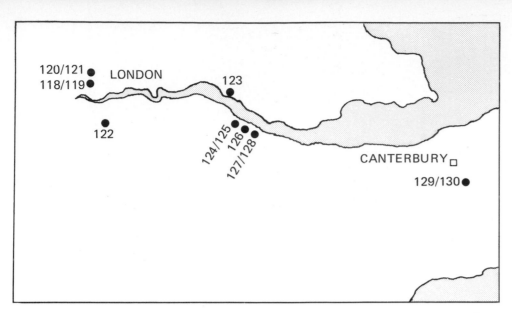

LONDON & THE SOUTH EAST

Plate 118 Just about visible from the main line out of Euston, Acton Lane Power Station has the distinction of operating the last steam locomotives, with any regularity in Greater London. *Little Barford* an 0-4-0ST built by Barclay (2069/1939) pauses at the end of the Saturday morning shift on 16th November, 1974.

Author

Plate 119 Acton Lane's other loco was very active over Christmas 1977. Robert Stephenson and Hawthorns 0-4-0ST, *Birkenhead* (7386/1948) plods over the Grand Union Canal with a train of coal for tipping on 23rd December of that year.
Author

Plate 120 London Transport-owned No. L94 (formerly GWR 7752) propels a Farringdon bound Sunday ballast train past Kings Cross (MET) on 6th July, 1969.

Victor C. K. Allen

Plate 121 Four ex-GWR 0-6-0PTs inside Neasden shed shortly before the end of steam on London Transport, which came on 6th June, 1971, marked by the familiar 'Last Day' scramble for photographs at a Neasden works open day.

Victor C. K. Allen

Plate 122 Unused for some time, this Peckett 0-4-0ST (2103/1950) was to be seen inside a tippler at C.E.G.B. Croydon 'B' Power Station on 26th November, 1975.

Author

Plate 123 Proctor and Gamble Ltd of West Thurrock in Essex could often be relied upon to steam one of their fireless steam loco-motives, usually a Bagnall 0-6-0F (2370/1929). However this was under repair in November 1974 when a Barclay 0-4-0F (1472/1916) was seen at work in the pouring rain. Both loco-motives have recently become redundant, following the arrival of a diesel replacement.

Author

Plate 124 A Barclay 0-4-0 fireless (2373/1956) strolls around the yard with a train of baled paper at the Imperial Paper Mills, Gravesend on 7th June, 1975. This locomotive has since been removed to the National Railway Museum collection at York.

Author

Plate 125 Two thirds of the locomotive stud at the Imperial Paper Mills, Gravesend were in steam on 7th June, 1975. Under charge is the Barclay (2373/1956), while another Barclay (1471/1916) passes by. An interesting point is that Barclay's next loco to be built, 1472 (Plate 123) worked just across the river Thames.

Author

STEAM IN KENT-1

Plate 126 This Barclay 0-4-0 fireless (1876/ 1925) is sadly not in use now. On 3rd November, 1977 she is seen outside her shed at Bowaters' Northfleet works, where she keeps company with two Ruston & Hornsby diesels.

Author

Plate 127 One of the problems for enthusiasts in studying a fleet of similar locos is that the parts carrying numbers often get swapped around. This practice could be found at the Swanscombe works of the Associated Portland Cement Manufacturers where running numbers were applied to easily removable saddle tanks. Hawthorn Leslie 0-4-0STs Nos. 3 and 4 rest between duties on 7th June, 1969.

Victor C. K. Allen

Plate 128 No. 4 trundles towards the quarry with a train of chalk empties.

Victor C. K. Allen

Plate 129 A neat looking Avonside 0-6-0ST, *St. Dunstan* (2004/1927) drags a loaded train from under the screens at Snowdown Colliery, Nonington, on 4th March, 1976.

Author

STEAM IN KENT-3

Plate 130 *St. Dunstan* again manoeuvring the same train out to the weighbridge next to the former S.E.C.R. Dover main line.

Author

LOCOMOTIVE BUILDERS

AB   *Andrew Barclay, Sons & Co. Ltd:* Plates 2, 6, 7, 8, 9, 10, 11, 12, 13, 14, 15, 16, 17, 18, 19, 20, 21, 22, 43, 52, 58, 63, 86, 87, 88, 100, 102, 103, 104, 117, 118, 123–126.

AE   *Avonside Engine Co. Ltd:* Plates 81, 84, 98, 129, 130.

BH   *Black, Hawthorn & Co. Ltd:* Plate 109.

BP   *Beyer, Peacock & Co. Ltd:* Plate 108.

GR   *Grant, Ritchie & Co:* Plate 13.

HC   *Hudswell, Clarke & Co. Ltd:* Plates 3, 45, 48, 49, 50, 56, 57, 82, 83, 95, 97, 99.

HE   *Hunslet Engine Co. Ltd:* Plates 27, 40, 44, 45, 51, 53, 58, 59, 60, 62, 65, 69, 72, 77, 78, 79, 115, 116.

HL   *R & W Hawthorn, Leslie & Co. Ltd:* Plates 41, 112, 117, 127, 128.

K   *Kitson & Co:* Plate 38.

KS   *Kerr, Stuart & Co. Ltd:* Plate 89.

Lill   *Lilleshall Co. Ltd:* Plate 107.

N   *Neilson & Co:* Plate 90.

P   *Peckett & Sons Ltd:* Plates 47, 54, 64, 70, 71, 76, 80, 81, 85, 86, 91, 110, 122.

RS   *Robert Stephenson & Co. Ltd:* Plates 34, 35, 38.

RSH   *Robert Stephenson & Hawthorns Ltd:* Plates 25, 26, 28, 29, 30, 39, 42, 55, 65, 66, 67, 68, 81, 105, 106, 119.

S   *Sentinel (Shrewsbury) Ltd:* Plates 4, 5.

Sdn   *Swindon Works, British Railways (Previously GWR).:* Plates 101, 120, 121.

VF   *Vulcan Foundry Ltd:* Plates 1, 23, 32, 33, 34, 37, 61, 62.

WB   *W. G. Bagnall Ltd:* Plates 72, 73, 74, 75, 94, 95, 111, 113, 114.